Mastering Your Budget

A Comprehensive Guide to Managing
Your Money

Max Reid

Table of Content

Introduction

As a young adult, I struggled with managing my finances. I had just landed my first job out of college, and I was excited to finally have a steady income. But as the months went by, I found myself constantly living paycheck to paycheck, with little to no savings and mounting credit card debt. I knew I needed to get my finances under control, but I didn't know where to start.

One day, while browsing through a bookstore, I stumbled upon a book on personal finance. It promised to teach me the skills I needed to master my budget and take control of my money. Intrigued, I picked it up and started reading. And that's when everything changed.

Over the next few months, I devoured every book and article on personal finance that I could get my hands on. I learned about budgeting, saving, investing, and more. I experimented with different strategies and tracked my progress. And slowly but surely, my financial situation began to improve.

Today, as a financial expert and author, I am passionate about sharing what I've learned with others. That's why I wrote "Mastering Your Budget: A Comprehensive Guide to Managing Your Money." Whether you're just starting out on your financial journey or you're looking to take your money management skills to the next level, this book has everything you need to succeed. So let's get started!

Why budgeting matters

Budgeting is an essential aspect of managing your finances. It is the process of creating a plan for your income and expenses, allowing you to track your money and make informed financial decisions. Many people tend to overlook the importance of budgeting and fail to realize the significant impact it can have on their financial well-being. Here are some reasons why budgeting matters:

Helps You Control Your Spending

Creating a budget helps you to track your expenses and control your spending. When you know exactly how much money you have coming in and going out, you can make informed decisions about where to spend your money. A budget can help you identify areas where you are overspending, allowing you to adjust your spending habits and save more money.

Allows You to Plan for the Future

Budgeting enables you to plan for the future and achieve your financial goals. Whether you want to buy a new car, save for a down payment on a house, or start a business, having a budget in place can help you achieve those goals. By creating a plan for your income and expenses, you can allocate money towards your goals and make progress towards achieving them.

Helps You Prepare for Emergencies

Unexpected expenses can arise at any time, and having a budget can help you prepare for them. By setting aside money for emergencies in your budget, you can avoid taking on debt or dipping into your savings when unexpected expenses occur. This can give you peace of mind and help you avoid financial stress.

Reduces Financial Stress

Budgeting can help you reduce financial stress by providing a sense of control over your money. When you have a plan in place for your income and expenses, you are less likely to feel overwhelmed by your finances. You can also avoid the stress that comes with living paycheck to paycheck or constantly worrying about money.

In conclusion, budgeting matters because it allows you to control your spending, plan for the future, prepare for emergencies, and reduce financial stress. By taking the time to create a budget and stick to it, you can improve your financial well-being and achieve your financial goals.

How this book can help you

"Mastering Your Budget: A Comprehensive Guide to Managing Your Money" is a book that can help you take control of your finances and achieve your financial goals. This book provides a step-by-step approach to budgeting and managing your money, making it easy for anyone to get started regardless of their level of financial knowledge. Here are some ways this book can help you:

Understand Your Finances

The book starts by helping you understand your current financial situation. It provides guidance on how to assess your financial situation, calculate your net worth, and identify your income and expenses. This information is essential for creating a budget that works for you.

Set Financial Goals

Once you have a clear understanding of your finances, the book helps you set financial goals. It provides strategies for creating SMART financial goals and prioritizing them based on your individual circumstances. By setting clear financial goals, you can focus your efforts and make progress towards achieving them.

Create a Budget

The book provides tips for creating a budget that works for you. It covers different types of budgets, such as zero-based budgeting and the envelope system, and helps you choose the one that suits your needs. It also provides guidance on how to track your budget and stay motivated to stick to it.

Manage Your Spending

The book provides strategies for managing your spending and reducing your expenses. It helps you avoid common budgeting mistakes and provides tips for staying motivated to stick to your budget. By managing your spending effectively, you can free up money to put towards your financial goals.

Maximize Your Income

The book also provides strategies for maximizing your income. It helps you identify ways to increase your income, such as negotiating a raise or promotion, and provides guidance on making the most of your benefits and perks.

Plan for the Future

The book helps you plan for the future by providing guidance on saving for emergencies, retirement planning, and investing basics. It provides practical advice for building a strong financial foundation and growing your net worth over time.

In conclusion, **"Mastering Your Budget: A Comprehensive Guide to Managing Your Money"** can help you take control of your finances and achieve your financial goals. Whether you are just starting out on your financial journey or looking to improve your current financial situation, this book provides the guidance and tools you need to succeed.

Chapter 1: Understanding Your Finances

Understanding your finances is an essential step towards achieving financial stability and success. It involves gaining a clear understanding of your income, expenses, debts, and assets. By understanding your finances, you can make informed financial decisions and create a plan to achieve your financial goals. Here are some key areas to consider when understanding your finances:

Income

Your income is the amount of money you earn from your job or other sources, such as rental income or investments. It is essential to have a clear understanding of your income to create a budget that works for you. Make sure to consider your net income, which is your income after taxes and deductions.

Expenses

Your expenses are the money you spend on essential and non-essential items, such as housing, food, transportation, entertainment, and other bills. It is crucial to identify your expenses and categorize them into fixed and variable expenses. Fixed expenses are the ones that stay the same every month, such as rent or mortgage payments, while variable expenses are those that can vary, such as groceries or entertainment.

Debts

Debts are the money you owe to others, such as credit card debt, student loans, or car loans. It is crucial to identify your debts, including the interest rates and monthly payments, to create a plan for paying them off. Make sure to prioritize your debts based on interest rates and payment terms.

Assets

Assets are the things you own, such as savings accounts, investments, and property. It is essential to identify your assets and determine their value to get a clear picture of your financial standing. Your assets can also help you achieve your financial goals by providing a source of income or by increasing in value over time.

Net Worth
Your net worth is the difference between your assets and liabilities. It is an essential measure of your financial health and can help you track your progress towards your financial goals. To calculate your net worth, subtract your liabilities from your assets.

In conclusion, understanding your finances involves gaining a clear understanding of your income, expenses, debts, assets, and net worth. By assessing these areas, you can create a plan to achieve your financial goals and make informed financial decisions. It is essential to regularly review and update your finances to ensure that you are on track towards financial stability and success.

Assessing your financial situation

Assessing your financial situation is an essential step towards achieving financial stability and success. It involves taking a close look at your income, expenses, debts, and assets to get a clear picture of your financial standing. By assessing your financial situation, you can identify areas that need improvement and create a plan to achieve your financial goals. Here are some steps to help you assess your financial situation:

Determine Your Net Worth
The first step in assessing your financial situation is to determine your net worth. This is the difference between your assets and liabilities. Your assets include things like your savings, investments, and property, while your liabilities include your debts, such as credit card balances, student loans, and

mortgages. Calculating your net worth will give you a clear understanding of your overall financial standing and help you set realistic goals for the future.

Analyze Your Income
Next, you should analyze your income to understand how much money you have coming in each month. This includes not just your salary, but also any additional sources of income, such as rental income or investments. Make sure to consider your net income, which is your income after taxes and deductions. Understanding your income will help you create a realistic budget and make informed financial decisions.

Track Your Expenses
To assess your financial situation, you also need to track your expenses. This means keeping track of everything you spend money on, from rent and utilities to groceries and entertainment. This will help you understand where your money is going

each month and identify areas where you can cut back. There are many tools available to help you track your expenses, from mobile apps to budgeting spreadsheets.

Identify Your Debts

Another important step in assessing your financial situation is identifying your debts. This includes credit card balances, student loans, car loans, and mortgages. Make a list of all your debts, including the interest rates and monthly payments. This will help you prioritize your debts and create a plan for paying them off.

Evaluate Your Assets

Finally, you should evaluate your assets to understand their value and how they can contribute to your overall financial situation. This includes savings accounts, investments, and property. Make sure to consider not just the value of your assets, but also how they are performing over time.

This will help you make informed decisions about your investments and ensure that your assets are helping you achieve your financial goals.

In conclusion, assessing your financial situation is an essential step towards achieving financial stability and success. By understanding your net worth, income, expenses, debts, and assets, you can create a plan to achieve your financial goals and make informed financial decisions. Regularly assessing your financial situation will help you stay on track and ensure that you are making progress towards a secure financial future.

Calculating your net worth

Calculating your net worth is an important step towards understanding your overall financial situation. It gives you an accurate picture of your financial health by taking into account all of your assets and liabilities. To calculate your net worth, follow these steps:

Determine Your Assets

Your assets include everything you own that has value, such as your savings accounts, investments, and property. Make a list of all your assets and determine their current value. For example, if you have a savings account, include the current balance. If you own property, include the estimated market value.

Determine Your Liabilities

Your liabilities include all the debts you owe, such as credit card balances, student loans, and mortgages. Make a list of all your liabilities and determine the total amount owed for each debt.

Calculate Your Net Worth

To calculate your net worth, subtract your total liabilities from your total assets. For example, if your assets total $500,000 and your liabilities total $200,000, your net worth is $300,000 ($500,000 - $200,000).

Keep in mind that your net worth can change over time based on changes in the value of your assets and the amount of debt you owe. It's important to regularly update your net worth calculation to ensure that you have an accurate understanding of your overall financial situation.

Calculating your net worth is an important tool for financial planning. It can help you understand your financial standing, set realistic financial goals, and make informed decisions about your finances. By regularly assessing your net worth, you can track your progress towards your financial goals and make adjustments as needed to achieve financial stability and success.

Identifying your income and expenses

Identifying your income and expenses is a crucial step in managing your finances effectively. It helps you understand where your money is coming from and where it's going, allowing you to make informed decisions about your spending and saving. Here are the steps to identify your income and expenses:

List Your Sources of Income
Start by making a list of all your sources of income. This includes your salary, any bonuses or commissions you receive, income from rental properties, and any other sources of income. Be sure to include all of your income sources to get a complete picture of your financial situation.

Determine Your Net Income
Once you've listed all of your income sources, determine your net income. This is the amount of money you have left after deducting taxes, Social Security, and any other deductions from your gross income. Your net income is what you actually have

available to use for your expenses and savings.

List Your Monthly Expenses
Make a list of all your monthly expenses, including rent or mortgage payments, utilities, transportation costs, groceries, insurance, and any other regular expenses. You can use past bank statements or credit card bills to help you identify all of your expenses.

Categorize Your Expenses
Categorize your expenses into fixed and variable expenses. Fixed expenses are regular monthly expenses that don't change, such as rent or mortgage payments. Variable expenses are costs that fluctuate, such as groceries and entertainment. This categorization will help you identify areas where you can cut back on spending to save money.

Total Your Expenses

Add up all of your monthly expenses to get your total monthly expenses. This will give you a clear understanding of how much money you need each month to cover your expenses.

Analyze Your Income and Expenses

Finally, analyze your income and expenses to understand your financial situation. Compare your net income to your total monthly expenses to see if you have a surplus or deficit each month. If you have a surplus, you can use the extra money to save for emergencies, pay off debt, or invest. If you have a deficit, you may need to reduce your expenses or find ways to increase your income.

Identifying your income and expenses is a crucial step in managing your finances effectively. By understanding your income and expenses, you can create a budget, set financial goals, and make informed decisions about your spending and saving. It's important to regularly review your income and expenses to ensure that you're on track to achieving your financial goals.

Chapter 2: Setting Financial Goals

Setting financial goals is an essential part of effective financial management. Financial goals provide a roadmap for your financial future and help you stay focused on your priorities. Here are the steps to set financial goals:

Define Your Goals

The first step in setting financial goals is to define what you want to achieve. Your goals should be specific, measurable, achievable, relevant, and time-bound (SMART). For example, you may want to save for a down payment on a house, pay off credit card debt, or build an emergency fund.

Determine the Cost

Once you've defined your goals, determine the cost of achieving them. This will help you understand how much you need to save and how long it will take to reach your goal.

Use tools such as budgeting spreadsheets or financial calculators to help you estimate the cost of achieving your goals.

Prioritize Your Goals

If you have multiple financial goals, prioritize them based on their importance and urgency. Consider the impact each goal will have on your financial situation and the time it will take to achieve each one. Prioritizing your goals will help you focus your efforts and resources on the most critical objectives.

Create a Plan

Once you've defined your goals, determined the cost, and prioritized them, create a plan to achieve them. Your plan should include specific action steps, timelines, and milestones to measure progress. You may need to adjust your budget, reduce expenses, or increase income to achieve your goals.

Track Your Progress

Regularly track your progress towards your goals. This will help you stay motivated and adjust your plan if necessary. Use tools such as financial apps or spreadsheets to help you monitor your progress and adjust your plan as needed.

Setting financial goals is a critical step in achieving financial stability and success. By defining your goals, determining the cost, prioritizing them, creating a plan, and tracking your progress, you can achieve your financial objectives and build a brighter financial future.

Creating SMART financial goals

Creating SMART financial goals is an effective way to achieve your financial objectives. SMART stands for Specific, Measurable, Achievable, Relevant, and Time-bound. Here's how to create SMART financial goals:

1. Specific: Your financial goals should be specific and well-defined. Rather than setting a general goal like "saving money," be specific about what you want to achieve, such as "saving $10,000 for a down payment on a house." The more specific your goal is, the easier it will be to measure your progress.

2. Measurable: Your financial goals should be measurable so you can track your progress. For example, if your goal is to pay off credit card debt, set a specific amount you want to pay off, such as $5,000. This will allow you to measure your progress towards achieving your goal.

3. Achievable: Your financial goals should be achievable based on your current financial situation. Consider your income, expenses, and other financial obligations when setting your

goals. While it's important to challenge yourself, setting unrealistic goals can lead to frustration and disappointment.

4. Relevant: Your financial goals should be relevant to your overall financial objectives. For example, if you want to retire early, saving for a down payment on a house may not be as relevant as investing in a retirement account. Ensure your financial goals align with your long-term financial objectives.

5. Time-bound: Your financial goals should have a specific timeline for completion. Setting a deadline will help you stay motivated and focused on achieving your goal. For example, if your goal is to save $10,000 for a down payment on a house, set a specific timeframe for achieving it, such as within 24 months.

By creating SMART financial goals, you can take control of your financial future and make significant progress towards achieving your financial objectives. Remember to regularly review and adjust your goals as needed to ensure you stay on track.

Prioritizing your goals

Prioritizing your goals is a critical step in achieving your financial objectives. Here are some tips to help you prioritize your financial goals:

1. Determine the Urgency of Each Goal: Some goals may be more urgent than others. For example, if you have credit card debt with high-interest rates, paying off that debt should be a priority over saving for a vacation.

2. Consider the Impact of Each Goal: Consider how achieving each goal will impact your overall financial situation. For example, building an emergency

fund may be more important than saving for a down payment on a house if you don't have any savings to cover unexpected expenses.

3. Evaluate the Costs of Each Goal: Determine the cost of achieving each goal and how it fits into your overall financial situation. Prioritize goals that are more affordable and feasible to achieve.

4. Align Goals with Your Values: Prioritize goals that align with your personal values and long-term objectives. For example, if you prioritize family time over career advancement, focus on goals that enable you to spend more time with your loved ones.

5. Break Goals into Smaller Steps: Break larger goals into smaller, more manageable steps. This will help you

stay motivated and make progress towards achieving your goals.

By prioritizing your financial goals, you can focus your efforts and resources on the most critical objectives. Remember to regularly review and adjust your goals as your financial situation changes and new opportunities arise.

Strategies for achieving your goals

Once you have set and prioritized your financial goals, it's time to develop a plan and strategies to achieve them. Here are some strategies for achieving your financial goals:

1. Create a Budget: A budget is a key tool in managing your finances and achieving your goals. By tracking your income and expenses, you can identify areas where you can reduce your spending and redirect those funds towards your goals.

2. Automate Savings: Set up automatic transfers to savings accounts, retirement accounts, or investment accounts to ensure that you are consistently making progress towards your goals.

3. Reduce Debt: High-interest debt can impede your progress towards achieving your financial goals. Prioritize paying off high-interest debt, such as credit card debt, as soon as possible.

4. Increase Income: Consider ways to increase your income, such as negotiating a raise or taking on a side hustle. The additional income can help you make faster progress towards your goals.

5. Invest Wisely: Investing can be an effective way to grow your wealth over

time. Educate yourself on different investment options and strategies to ensure you are making smart investment decisions.

6. Be Patient and Persistent: Achieving financial goals takes time and effort. Be patient and persistent in your efforts, and don't be discouraged by setbacks or slow progress.

By following these strategies, you can make steady progress towards achieving your financial goals. Remember to regularly review and adjust your plan as needed to ensure you stay on track.

Chapter 3: Creating a Budget

Creating a budget is an essential step in managing your finances and achieving your financial goals. Here are the steps to create a budget:

1. Track Your Income: Start by tracking your income, including all sources such as your salary, side hustles, or investment income.

2. List Your Expenses: Make a list of all your monthly expenses, including fixed expenses such as rent or mortgage payments, utilities, and insurance, as well as variable expenses such as groceries, entertainment, and transportation.

3. Categorize Your Expenses: Categorize your expenses into different categories, such as housing,

food, transportation, and entertainment.

4. Determine Your Net Income: Subtract your total expenses from your total income to determine your net income. If your expenses exceed your income, you may need to find ways to cut back on expenses or increase your income.

5. Set Goals: Set financial goals for yourself, such as paying off debt or saving for a down payment on a home. Allocate a portion of your budget towards achieving those goals.

6. Monitor and Adjust: Monitor your budget regularly to ensure that you are staying on track. Adjust your budget as needed to accommodate changes in your income or expenses.

7. Use Budgeting Tools: Consider using budgeting tools, such as budgeting

apps or spreadsheets, to help you track your income and expenses.

Creating a budget can help you identify areas where you can reduce your spending and redirect those funds towards your financial goals. By sticking to your budget and regularly monitoring your progress, you can make steady progress towards achieving your financial objectives.

Different types of budgets

There are several types of budgets that you can use to manage your finances. Here are some of the most common types of budgets:

1. Zero-Based Budget: A zero-based budget is a budgeting method where you allocate every dollar of income towards a specific expense or financial goal. This type of budget can help you prioritize your spending and make the most of your income.

2. Envelope Budget: An envelope budget is a budgeting method where you allocate cash into different envelopes for each expense category. This method can help you control your spending and avoid overspending in certain categories.

3. 50/30/20 Budget: The 50/30/20 budget is a budgeting method that divides your income into three categories: 50% for needs, 30% for wants, and 20% for savings and debt payments.

4. Rolling Budget: A rolling budget is a budget that is updated continuously based on actual spending and income. This type of budget can help you adjust your spending and savings goals as your financial situation changes.

5. Annual Budget: An annual budget is a budget that covers an entire year. This type of budget can help you plan for long-term financial goals and expenses, such as a down payment on a home or a major vacation.

6. Project-Based Budget: A project-based budget is a budget that is specific to a particular project or goal, such as a home renovation or starting a business.

Ultimately, the type of budget you choose will depend on your financial goals, spending habits, and personal preferences. Consider experimenting with different budgeting methods to find the one that works best for you.

Tips for creating a successful budget

Creating a budget can be a valuable tool in helping you achieve your financial goals. Here are some tips to help you create a successful budget:

1. Set Realistic Goals: Make sure your goals are realistic and achievable based on your income and expenses. Be specific about what you want to achieve and create a timeline to help you stay on track.

2. Track Your Expenses: Keep track of your expenses for at least a month to identify your spending patterns and areas where you can cut back. Use a spreadsheet or a budgeting app to help you track your expenses.

3. Include All Expenses: Be sure to include all of your expenses, including

small ones like coffee or snacks. These expenses can add up over time and affect your overall budget.

4. Prioritize Your Spending: Allocate your funds towards your most important expenses and financial goals. For example, prioritize saving for an emergency fund or paying off high-interest debt.

5. Be Flexible: Your budget should be flexible to allow for unexpected expenses or changes in income. Leave some wiggle room in your budget for unexpected expenses.

6. Review and Adjust Regularly: Review your budget regularly and adjust as needed. Life circumstances, such as a job loss or a new baby, may require you to adjust your budget.

7. Get Support: Share your budget goals with a friend or family member who can provide support and hold you accountable.

Remember, creating a budget is just the first step in achieving your financial goals. Sticking to your budget and making adjustments as necessary is key to success.

Tracking your budget

Tracking your budget is an important step in ensuring that you stay on track with your financial goals. Here are some tips for tracking your budget effectively:

1. Use a Budgeting App: Consider using a budgeting app, such as Mint or YNAB, to help you track your expenses and monitor your budget. These apps can link to your bank accounts and credit cards to automatically track your spending.

2. Set Reminders: Set reminders to update your budget regularly. This can help you stay on top of your spending and make adjustments as needed.
3. Keep Receipts: Keep receipts for all of your purchases so you can enter them into your budgeting app or spreadsheet. This can also help you identify any errors or discrepancies in your budget.
4. Review Regularly: Review your budget regularly to ensure that you are staying on track with your financial goals. This can help you identify areas where you may be overspending or where you can cut back.
5. Be Honest: Be honest with yourself about your spending habits. Don't underestimate your expenses or try to justify overspending. This can prevent you from achieving your financial goals.
6. Track Savings: Track your savings and debt payments to see how much

progress you are making towards your financial goals. Celebrate small victories to stay motivated.

Remember, tracking your budget is not a one-time task. It is an ongoing process that requires regular monitoring and adjustments. With consistency and dedication, tracking your budget can help you achieve your financial goals and lead a more financially stable life.

Chapter 4: Managing Your Spending

Managing your spending is an essential part of achieving your financial goals. Here are some tips to help you manage your spending:

1. Create a Budget: Create a budget that includes all of your income and expenses. This will help you identify areas where you can cut back on spending and prioritize your financial goals.

2. Separate Needs from Wants: Distinguish between your essential needs, such as food and shelter, and your discretionary wants, such as entertainment or luxury items. Prioritize your needs first and allocate funds towards your wants after taking care of your necessities.

3. Shop Smart: Compare prices and shop around before making big purchases. Look for discounts, coupons, and sales to help you save money.

4. Avoid Impulse Purchases: Try to avoid impulse purchases by creating a shopping list and sticking to it. Wait a day or two before making a purchase to make sure it is something you truly need or want.

5. Use Cash: Consider using cash for your discretionary spending. This can help you stay within your budget and avoid overspending.

6. Monitor Your Credit Cards: If you use credit cards, monitor your balances and pay them off in full each month to avoid high-interest charges.

7. Automate Savings: Consider automating your savings by setting up automatic transfers to a savings account or investment account. This can help you save money without even thinking about it.

Remember, managing your spending is an ongoing process. It requires discipline, patience, and consistency. With time and effort, you can develop good spending habits and achieve your financial goals.

Strategies for reducing expenses

Reducing expenses is an important step in achieving your financial goals. Here are some strategies for reducing your expenses:

1. Cut Out Unnecessary Expenses: Review your expenses and identify any unnecessary or excessive expenses. These may include subscriptions or memberships that you no longer use or rarely use.

2. Lower Monthly Bills: Negotiate with your service providers for lower bills. You can call your cable or internet provider to see if there are any promotional rates available or switch to a different provider to save money.

3. Save on Groceries: Reduce your grocery bills by creating a meal plan, shopping with a list, and buying generic or store-brand products instead of name brands.

4. Reduce Transportation Costs: Consider carpooling, biking, or walking instead of driving alone. This can help you save money on gas and car maintenance.

5. Cut Back on Dining Out: Reduce your dining out expenses by cooking at home more often or packing your lunch for work. You can also look for

restaurant deals or coupons to save money when you dine out.

6. Review Insurance Policies: Review your insurance policies to see if you can lower your premiums. You can increase your deductible to reduce your monthly payments or shop around for better rates.

7. Use Energy-Efficient Appliances: Switch to energy-efficient appliances and light bulbs to lower your energy bills. You can also reduce your water usage by taking shorter showers or installing low-flow showerheads.

Remember, reducing expenses is not a one-time task. It requires ongoing effort and discipline to stick to your budget and prioritize your financial goals. By adopting good spending habits and making smart choices, you can reduce your expenses and achieve financial stability.

Avoiding common budgeting mistakes

Budgeting is a critical part of managing your finances, and making mistakes can derail your progress towards your financial goals. Here are some common budgeting mistakes to avoid:

1. Not Tracking Expenses: If you don't track your expenses, you won't know where your money is going, making it difficult to create an effective budget. Use a budgeting app or spreadsheet to track your expenses and stay on top of your finances.

2. Setting Unrealistic Goals: Setting unrealistic goals can make it challenging to stick to your budget. Be honest with yourself about what you can realistically afford and set achievable goals that align with your income and expenses.

3. Failing to Prioritize Debt Repayment: If you have debt, prioritize paying it off before allocating money to other expenses. High-interest debt can quickly accumulate, making it difficult to achieve other financial goals.

4. Not Building an Emergency Fund: Unexpected expenses can arise at any time, and without an emergency fund, you may have to dip into your savings or go into debt to cover them. Build an emergency fund by setting aside a portion of your income each month.

5. Ignoring Infrequent Expenses: Infrequent expenses, such as annual insurance premiums or car maintenance costs, can throw off your budget if you don't account for them. Anticipate these expenses and set aside money for them each month.

6. Overlooking Small Expenses: Small expenses, such as daily coffee or snack purchases, can add up over time and impact your budget. Track your small expenses and consider cutting back on unnecessary purchases.

7. Failing to Adjust Your Budget: Your financial situation may change over time, so it's important to adjust your budget accordingly. Review your budget regularly and make adjustments as needed.

Remember, budgeting is a process, and it may take time to develop good habits and avoid common mistakes. Be patient, stay disciplined, and learn from your mistakes to achieve your financial goals.

Staying motivated to stick to your budget

Sticking to a budget can be challenging, especially when unexpected expenses arise or when you need to make sacrifices to meet your financial goals. Here are some tips to help you stay motivated and on track:

1. Visualize Your Goals: Keep your financial goals in mind and visualize what achieving them will look and feel like. Whether it's paying off debt, saving for a vacation, or building an emergency fund, having a clear picture of your goals can help you stay motivated.

2. Celebrate Small Wins: Celebrate the small milestones you reach along the way. Whether it's paying off a credit card or sticking to your budget for a week, take time to acknowledge your

progress and feel proud of your achievements.

3. Stay Accountable: Share your financial goals and budget with a friend or family member who can help hold you accountable. Consider joining a support group or online community to connect with others who are also working towards financial stability.

4. Find Alternative Rewards: Instead of relying on shopping or dining out as a reward for sticking to your budget, find alternative ways to treat yourself. This could include taking a walk, reading a book, or indulging in a hobby.

5. Focus on the Long-Term: Remember that sticking to your budget is an investment in your future. Keeping your long-term financial goals in mind

can help you stay motivated and committed to your budget.

6. Keep Your Budget Realistic: If your budget is too strict or unrealistic, it can be difficult to stick to it. Make sure your budget is achievable and includes room for unexpected expenses or emergencies.

7. Learn from Your Mistakes: If you make a mistake or overspend, don't get discouraged. Use it as an opportunity to learn and adjust your budget moving forward.

Remember, staying motivated to stick to your budget is a continuous process. With practice and persistence, you can develop good habits and achieve your financial goals.

Chapter 5: Maximizing Your Income

Maximizing your income is an essential part of achieving financial stability and meeting your financial goals. Here are some strategies for increasing your income:

1. Negotiate Your Salary: If you're employed, negotiate your salary to ensure you're being paid fairly for your skills and experience. Do your research on the average salary for your position and be prepared to make a case for your value to the company.

2. Consider a Side Hustle: A side hustle can provide an additional source of income and help you achieve your financial goals faster. Consider freelancing, selling items online, or offering a service based on your skills or interests.

3. Take on Overtime or Additional Shifts: If you're employed, consider taking on overtime or additional shifts to earn extra income. Make sure to factor in the additional income when creating or adjusting your budget.

4. Pursue Higher Education or Training: Pursuing higher education or training can lead to career advancement and increased earning potential. Research programs or certifications that can help you achieve your career goals and increase your income.

5. Invest in the Stock Market: Investing in the stock market can provide a potential source of passive income. Research and consult with a financial advisor to make informed investment decisions based on your financial goals and risk tolerance.

6. Rent Out a Room or Property: If you have a spare room or property, consider renting it out on a short-term or long-term basis to generate additional income.

Remember, increasing your income requires effort and dedication, but it can pay off in the long run by providing more financial freedom and helping you achieve your goals faster.

Strategies for increasing your income

Making the most of your benefits and perks In addition to your salary or wages, your employer may offer a variety of benefits and perks that can help you save money and improve your quality of life. Here are some ways to make the most of your benefits and perks:

1. Health Benefits: Take advantage of your employer's health benefits, such as medical, dental, and vision insurance. Make sure you understand the coverage and any out-of-pocket expenses. Consider enrolling in a flexible spending account (FSA) or health savings account (HSA) to save money on medical expenses.

2. Retirement Benefits: Participate in your employer's retirement plan, such as a 401(k) or pension. Contribute as much as you can afford, and consider taking advantage of any matching contributions from your employer.

3. Wellness Programs: Many employers offer wellness programs that can help you save money on healthcare costs and improve your overall health. Take advantage of these programs, which may include gym memberships,

wellness classes, and health coaching.

4. Paid Time Off: Make sure you take advantage of your paid time off, including vacation days and sick days. Use this time to recharge and take care of your physical and mental health.

5. Discounts and Perks: Many employers offer discounts and perks on products and services, such as gym memberships, cell phone plans, and entertainment. Take advantage of these discounts to save money on things you already use or enjoy.

6. Professional Development: Some employers offer professional development opportunities, such as training and conferences. Take advantage of these opportunities to

improve your skills and advance your career.

Remember, your benefits and perks can help you save money and improve your quality of life. Take the time to understand and maximize the benefits and perks offered by your employer.

Negotiating a raise or promotion

Negotiating a raise or promotion can be nerve-wracking, but it's an important step to increase your income and advance your career. Here are some tips for negotiating a raise or promotion:

1. Do your research: Research your industry and position to determine what the average salary or compensation is. Use online resources, such as Glassdoor or Payscale, to gather data and compare your salary to industry averages.

2. Build a case: Make a list of your accomplishments and contributions to the company. Highlight how you have exceeded expectations and added value to the organization. Use specific examples and data to support your case.

3. Practice your pitch: Practice your negotiation pitch in advance. Anticipate potential objections and be prepared to address them. Consider rehearsing with a friend or mentor.

4. Schedule a meeting: Schedule a meeting with your supervisor to discuss your salary or promotion. Be prepared to discuss your accomplishments and contributions, and make your case for a raise or promotion.

5. Be open to compromise: Consider alternatives to a salary increase or

promotion, such as flexible scheduling, additional vacation days, or professional development opportunities.

6. Follow up: If your negotiation is successful, be sure to get the agreement in writing and follow up with any necessary paperwork. If your negotiation is not successful, ask for feedback and a plan to work towards a future raise or promotion.

Remember, negotiating a raise or promotion requires preparation, confidence, and a willingness to advocate for yourself. With these tips, you can increase your chances of a successful negotiation and advance your career.

Chapter 6: Planning for the Future

Planning for the future is an important part of managing your money. Here are some key areas to consider when creating a long-term financial plan:

1. Retirement: It's never too early to start planning for retirement. Consider your retirement goals and estimate how much money you will need to save to achieve them. Consider contributing to a 401(k), IRA, or other retirement savings account to take advantage of tax benefits and compound interest.

2. Emergency Fund: Set aside money for unexpected expenses or emergencies, such as car repairs or medical bills. Aim to save 3-6 months of living expenses in an emergency fund.

3. Estate Planning: Plan for the distribution of your assets after your death. Consider creating a will, naming beneficiaries for your retirement accounts and life insurance policies, and establishing a trust if necessary.

4. Insurance: Protect yourself and your loved ones with insurance, such as health insurance, life insurance, and disability insurance. Review your insurance coverage annually to ensure you have adequate protection.

5. Education: If you or your children plan to pursue higher education, consider setting up a 529 college savings plan to save for tuition and other expenses.

6. Charitable Giving: Consider giving back to your community or supporting causes you care about through charitable giving. Research

organizations and causes you are interested in and set a budget for your donations.

Remember, a long-term financial plan requires ongoing monitoring and adjustments. Review your plan annually and make changes as necessary to stay on track towards your financial goals.

Saving for emergencies

Saving for emergencies is an essential part of financial planning. An emergency fund is a reserve of money set aside to cover unexpected expenses, such as a medical emergency, job loss, or car repair. Here are some steps to help you save for emergencies:

1. Set a savings goal: Determine how much money you need to set aside in your emergency fund. Aim to save 3-6 months of living expenses.

2. Create a budget: Track your income and expenses to determine how much money you can afford to save each month. Look for areas where you can cut expenses to free up more money for savings.

3. Choose a savings account: Look for a savings account with a high interest rate and no fees. Consider setting up automatic transfers from your checking account to your savings account each month.

4. Build your emergency fund: Start saving regularly and consistently. Make it a priority to add to your emergency fund each month, even if it's a small amount.

5. Use your emergency fund wisely: Only use your emergency fund for true emergencies, such as unexpected medical expenses or a job loss. Avoid

dipping into your emergency fund for non-essential expenses.

Remember, building an emergency fund takes time and discipline. Start small and be consistent. Over time, your emergency fund will grow, giving you peace of mind and financial security.

Retirement planning

Retirement planning is an essential part of financial planning. Here are some steps to help you prepare for a comfortable retirement:

1. Determine your retirement goals: Consider the lifestyle you want to have in retirement and estimate how much money you will need to save to achieve those goals.

2. Estimate your retirement income: Calculate how much income you will receive from Social Security,

pensions, and other sources of retirement income.

3. Create a retirement savings plan: Determine how much money you need to save each month to reach your retirement goals. Consider contributing to a 401(k), IRA, or other retirement savings account to take advantage of tax benefits and compound interest.

4. Invest wisely: Consider investing in a diversified portfolio of stocks, bonds, and other assets to maximize your retirement savings. Consult with a financial advisor to develop an investment strategy that is appropriate for your risk tolerance and retirement goals.

5. Review and adjust your plan: Review your retirement plan annually and make adjustments as necessary to

stay on track towards your retirement goals.

Remember, the earlier you start saving for retirement, the better. Even small contributions made over time can grow into a significant retirement savings. Consult with a financial advisor to develop a retirement plan that is tailored to your individual needs and goals.

Investing basics

Investing is an important part of building wealth over time. Here are some basic concepts to understand before you start investing:

1. Diversification: Diversification means spreading your investments across different asset classes, such as stocks, bonds, and real estate, to reduce the risk of losing money in any one investment.

2. Risk and return: Every investment carries some level of risk, but the potential return on investment is generally higher for riskier investments. Understanding your risk tolerance is important in selecting investments that match your investment objectives.

3. Asset allocation: Asset allocation refers to the process of dividing your investments among different asset classes based on your investment goals, risk tolerance, and time horizon.

4. Buy and hold strategy: Buy and hold is an investment strategy where investors buy stocks or other assets and hold onto them for the long-term, usually years or decades. This strategy can help reduce transaction costs and taxes and allows investors

to benefit from the long-term growth of their investments.

5. Cost of investing: Every investment has costs associated with it, including transaction fees, management fees, and taxes. Understanding these costs is important in selecting investments that will maximize your return on investment.

Remember, investing can be complex, and it's important to do your research and consult with a financial advisor before making any investment decisions. Start by understanding your investment objectives, risk tolerance, and time horizon, and create a diversified portfolio that aligns with your goals.

Chapter 7: Managing Debt

Managing debt is an important part of financial planning. Here are some strategies for managing debt:

1. Create a debt payoff plan: Start by listing all of your debts, including the balance, interest rate, and minimum payment. Determine which debt has the highest interest rate and focus on paying it off first while making minimum payments on other debts. Once that debt is paid off, move on to the next highest interest rate debt and so on.

2. Consider debt consolidation: Debt consolidation involves combining multiple debts into a single loan with a lower interest rate. This can make it easier to manage your debt and save money on interest charges.

3. Prioritize high-interest debt: High-interest debt, such as credit card debt, should be prioritized over low-interest debt, such as a mortgage. Paying off high-interest debt first can save you money on interest charges over time.

4. Negotiate with creditors: If you're struggling to make payments, reach out to your creditors and ask about options for reducing your interest rate or monthly payments. They may be willing to work with you to create a more manageable payment plan.

5. Avoid taking on new debt: While paying off existing debt, avoid taking on new debt, such as credit card balances or personal loans. This can make it more difficult to get out of debt and prolong the time it takes to become financially stable.

Remember, managing debt takes time and effort. It's important to stay committed to your debt payoff plan and avoid taking on new debt to ensure long-term financial success.

Understanding your debt

Understanding your debt is the first step in managing it effectively. Here are some things to consider when looking at your debt:

1. Types of debt: There are two main types of debt: secured and unsecured. Secured debt is backed by collateral, such as a car or house, and is typically associated with lower interest rates. Unsecured debt, such as credit card debt or personal loans, does not require collateral and often has higher interest rates.

2. Interest rates: Interest rates determine how much you pay in interest charges

over time. High interest rates can make it difficult to pay off debt, while low interest rates can help you save money on interest charges.

3. Payment terms: Payment terms refer to the length of time you have to repay your debt. Longer repayment terms may result in lower monthly payments but can also lead to paying more in interest charges over time.

4. Minimum payments: Minimum payments are the minimum amount required each month to avoid defaulting on your debt. However, making only minimum payments can result in paying more in interest charges over time and prolong the time it takes to pay off the debt.

5. Total debt amount: Knowing the total amount of debt you owe can help you

create a debt payoff plan and set realistic goals for becoming debt-free.

Understanding these factors can help you make informed decisions about how to manage your debt and create a plan for paying it off. It's important to regularly review your debt and make adjustments to your plan as needed to ensure you stay on track towards financial stability.

Strategies for paying off debt

Paying off debt can be a challenging process, but with the right strategies in place, it is possible to make progress towards becoming debt-free. Here are some strategies for paying off debt:

1. Create a budget: Creating a budget can help you identify areas where you can cut back on spending and redirect those funds towards paying off debt. By tracking your income and expenses, you can prioritize debt

payments and make sure you are making progress towards your goals.

2. Snowball or avalanche method: These are two popular debt payoff methods. The snowball method involves paying off your smallest debt first, then moving on to the next smallest debt, while the avalanche method involves prioritizing debts with the highest interest rates first. Both methods can be effective, and it's important to choose the method that works best for your individual circumstances.

3. Increase your income: Finding ways to increase your income, such as taking on a side hustle or negotiating a raise, can help you put more money towards debt payments.

4. Refinance or consolidate debt: Refinancing or consolidating debt can help you lower your interest rates and

reduce your monthly payments, making it easier to pay off debt over time.

5. Seek professional help: If you are struggling with debt, seeking the help of a financial advisor or credit counseling service can provide you with personalized guidance and support.

Remember, paying off debt takes time and effort, but with a clear plan in place and the right strategies, you can make progress towards becoming debt-free and achieving financial freedom.

Avoiding and managing debt in the future

Avoiding and managing debt in the future is an essential part of achieving long-term financial stability. Here are some strategies to help you avoid and manage debt in the future:

1. Live below your means: One of the most effective ways to avoid debt is to live below your means. This means being mindful of your spending and making sure you are not spending more than you can afford.

2. Build an emergency fund: Having an emergency fund can help you avoid going into debt in case of unexpected expenses or emergencies. Aim to have at least three to six months of living expenses saved in an emergency fund.

3. Use credit responsibly: Using credit cards responsibly can help you build a good credit history and avoid accumulating debt. Only charge what you can afford to pay off in full each

month, and avoid carrying a balance and paying high interest rates.

4. Prioritize saving for big purchases: Instead of going into debt for big purchases like a car or home, prioritize saving up for these purchases. This may require delaying gratification and making short-term sacrifices, but it can help you avoid debt in the long run.

5. Seek professional help if needed: If you find yourself struggling with debt again, don't hesitate to seek professional help from a financial advisor or credit counseling service. These professionals can help you develop a plan to manage your debt and achieve financial stability.

By following these strategies and making smart financial decisions, you can avoid and manage debt in the future and achieve long-term financial success.

Chapter 8: Building Wealth

Building wealth is a long-term goal that requires discipline, hard work, and smart financial decisions. Here are some strategies to help you build wealth:

1. Invest in your education and skills: Investing in your education and skills can help you increase your earning potential and open up new opportunities for career advancement.

2. Live below your means: Living below your means and being mindful of your spending can help you save money and invest more for your future.

3. Maximize your retirement savings: Contributing to a retirement account like a 401(k) or IRA can help you build wealth over time through compound interest.

4. Diversify your investments: Diversifying your investments can help you manage risk and maximize your returns. Consider investing in a mix of stocks, bonds, and other assets that align with your goals and risk tolerance.

5. Start a side hustle or business: Starting a side hustle or business can help you increase your income and build wealth over time. Look for opportunities to monetize your skills or hobbies, and consider investing profits back into your business or other investments.

6. Seek professional advice: Consulting with a financial advisor can help you develop a personalized plan to achieve your financial goals and build wealth over time.

Remember that building wealth takes time and requires patience and perseverance. By following these strategies and making smart financial decisions, you can build wealth and achieve financial freedom over time.

Investing for long-term wealth

Investing for long-term wealth is a great way to achieve financial independence and build a comfortable retirement. Here are some strategies to consider when investing for the long-term:

1. Diversify your portfolio: Diversification is key to long-term investing success. Spread your investments across a variety of asset classes, including stocks, bonds, real estate, and alternative investments such as commodities and cryptocurrencies.

2. Invest regularly: Consistent investing over time is essential to building long-term wealth. Consider setting up

automatic investments or contributing to your investment portfolio on a regular basis.

3. Consider low-cost index funds: Index funds offer low fees and diversification, making them a popular choice for long-term investors. Consider investing in a mix of domestic and international index funds to spread your risk.

4. Rebalance your portfolio regularly: Rebalancing your portfolio on a regular basis can help you maintain a diversified mix of assets and minimize risk. Consider rebalancing your portfolio at least once a year or when market conditions warrant a change.

5. Stay the course: Long-term investing requires patience and discipline. Avoid reacting to short-term market volatility and focus on your long-term goals.

Remember, time in the market is more important than timing the market.

6. Consult with a financial advisor: A financial advisor can help you develop a long-term investment plan that aligns with your goals, risk tolerance, and time horizon. Consider seeking the advice of a trusted financial professional to help guide your investment decisions.

Investing for long-term wealth requires a long-term perspective, a diversified portfolio, and a disciplined approach to investing. By following these strategies, you can work towards achieving your long-term financial goals and building a comfortable retirement.

Growing your net worth over time

Growing your net worth over time is an important part of building long-term wealth and achieving financial independence. Here are some strategies to consider when looking to increase your net worth:

1. Save aggressively: Saving as much as you can is the foundation of building wealth. Consider increasing your savings rate by reducing expenses, increasing income, and maximizing tax-advantaged accounts such as 401(k)s and IRAs.

2. Invest wisely: Investing is a key driver of long-term wealth accumulation. Consider diversifying your investments, investing in low-cost index funds, and rebalancing your portfolio regularly to maximize returns and minimize risk.

3. Pay off high-interest debt: High-interest debt can be a drag on your net worth over time. Consider paying off credit card debt and other high-interest loans as quickly as

possible to free up more of your income for savings and investments.

4. Own a home: Homeownership can be a great way to build equity and increase your net worth over time. Consider buying a home in a desirable area with good potential for appreciation and make sure to factor in all the costs associated with owning a home when deciding if it's the right choice for you.

5. Build multiple income streams: Multiple income streams can help you diversify your income and increase your earning potential over time. Consider starting a side hustle, investing in rental properties, or pursuing passive income streams such as dividend-paying stocks or real estate investment trusts (REITs).

6. Continuously educate yourself: Investing in yourself and your education can pay off in big ways over time. Continuously learning new skills and expanding your knowledge can increase your earning potential and help you make better financial decisions.

Growing your net worth over time requires a long-term perspective, discipline, and a commitment to continually learning and improving. By following these strategies and focusing on your long-term goals, you can work towards achieving financial independence and building a comfortable retirement.

Conclusion

Managing your money effectively is a key component of achieving financial success and security. By assessing your financial situation, setting SMART financial goals, creating a budget, and managing your spending and debt, you can build a strong foundation for long-term financial stability. Additionally, investing wisely, saving aggressively, and continuously educating yourself can help you grow your net worth over time and build the wealth necessary to achieve your financial goals. By following the strategies outlined in this book and staying committed to your long-term financial plan, you can take control of your finances and achieve financial independence.

Reviewing your progress

Regularly reviewing your progress is an important part of achieving your financial goals. By tracking your spending, saving, and investment performance, you can identify areas where you may need to adjust your strategy or make changes to your budget. This can help you stay on track towards your financial goals and make any necessary adjustments to ensure you reach them.

During your progress reviews, be sure to celebrate any successes you have achieved along the way, and don't get discouraged if you haven't achieved all of your goals yet. Remember that building financial stability and wealth takes time, and it's important to stay committed to your financial plan and continue making progress towards your goals.

Continuing to master your budget

Mastering your budget is an ongoing process that requires ongoing effort and attention. Here are some tips for continuing to improve your financial management skills:

1. Stay committed to your financial goals: Revisit your financial goals regularly and stay committed to achieving them. This will help you stay motivated and focused on your long-term financial success.

2. Keep learning: Continue to educate yourself about personal finance and investing. Read books and articles, attend workshops and webinars, and seek the advice of financial professionals to help you make informed financial decisions.

3. Stay disciplined: Stick to your budget and avoid overspending. This will help you avoid debt and stay on track towards achieving your financial goals.

4. Adjust your strategy as needed: Be flexible and willing to adjust your financial strategy as needed. Life

circumstances and financial goals can change, so be prepared to adjust your strategy accordingly.

5. Build an emergency fund: Continue to build your emergency fund to protect yourself from unexpected financial emergencies.

6. Invest wisely: Invest your money wisely to maximize your long-term financial growth potential.

By following these tips and staying committed to mastering your budget, you can achieve financial security and independence and build the wealth necessary to achieve your long-term financial goals.

www.ingramcontent.com/pod-product-compliance
Lightning Source LLC
Chambersburg PA
CBHW072149230526
45467CB00042B/1433